PET OWNER'S GUIDE TO THE
TORTOISE

Simon J. Girling
BVMS CertZooMed MRCVS

RINGPRESS

ABOUT THE AUTHOR

Simon Girling became a Member of the Royal College of Veterinary Surgeons after graduating with honours from Glasgow Veterinary School in 1994. He spent a brief time in mixed practice in Cumbria before setting up a first opinion and referral centre for exotic species at the Braid Veterinary Hospital in Edinburgh.

Simon gained the Royal College of Veterinary Surgeons Certificate in Zoological Medicine in 1999 when he also became a Member of the Institute of Biology and a Chartered Biologist. He is currently the Honorary Treasurer of the British Veterinary Zoological Society and involved in animal welfare aspects of the Royal Zoological Society of Scotland. He is also a member of the Association of Reptilian and Amphibian Veterinarians, the British Chelonia Group, the Association of Avian Veterinarians and the American Association of Zoo Veterinarians.

PHOTOGRAPHY
Fred Holmes

Published by Ringpress Books,
A Division of INTERPET LTD
Vincent Lane, Dorking, Surrey RH4 3YX

First published 2002
©2002 Ringpress Books. All rights reserved

Design: Rob Benson

ISBN 1 86054 119 4

Printed and bound in Hong Kong through Printworks International Ltd.

CONTENTS

1

INTRODUCING THE TORTOISE 18

Pets; Preservation; International protection; Ownership; The shell (Structure; Trauma); Respiration; The digestive system; The urinary system; The reproductive system; Temperature control; Life-expectancy.

2

TORTOISE SPECIES 13

Mediterranean species (Spur-Thighed Tortoise; Hermann's Tortoise, Marginated Tortoise, Horsfield's Tortoise); Non-Mediterranean species (Leopard Tortoise; African Spurred Tortoise; Indian Starred Tortoise; Chaco Tortoise; Red-Footed Tortoise; Yellow-Footed Tortoise).

3

CHOOSING YOUR TORTOISE 22

Responsibility; Vendors; What species? (Mediterranean; Non-Mediterranean; Exotic); Male or Female?; Sexing; Numbers; (Mixing sexes; Mixing species); Children; Pets; Carriers; Handling.

4

TORTOISE ACCOMMODATION 33

Mediterranean species (Outdoor shelters; Indoor housing); Non-Mediterranean species (Outdoors; Indoor housing).

GENERAL CARE   **42**

Shell care (Dehydration; Bathing);
Environment; Hibernation; Post-
hibernation; Behaviour (Adults;
Juveniles; Problems; Accidents).

NUTRITION   **51**

No meat; Mastication; Digestion; Water; Suitable plants
(Variety; Caution; Tortoise pellets); Dietary problems; A proper
menu; Poisonous plants.

BREEDING TORTOISES   **59**

Preparation; Timing; Introductions; Courtship; Female care
(Mediterraneans; South Americans); Incubation (The
incubator; Sex-determination); Hatchlings; Youngsters;
Reproductive problems.

HEALTH CARE   **72**

Warning signs; Common diseases
(Shell problems; Skin ailments;
Beaks; Deformities); Breathing
problems; Digestive problems
(Diarrhoea; Constipation,
Anorexia; Colic; Vomiting; Liver
problems); Neurological
indications; Lameness; Eyes;
Zoonotic diseases.

1
Introducing The Tortoise

The difficulty about writing a book on tortoises is that the word 'tortoise' means different things to different people. In the UK, it refers to any member of the shelled reptile family inhabiting dry land. Marine species are called turtles and freshwater species are known as terrapins. In the USA, all shelled reptiles are referred to as turtles or terrapins, whether aquatic or not. In Australia, all bar one of the native turtles are referred to as tortoises.

For the purposes of this book the term 'tortoise' will refer to any

The first tortoises were brought back to the UK by Charles Darwin, and, ever since that time, tortoise-keeping has been a popular hobby.

land-based shelled reptile. The technical name for shelled reptiles is Chelonia. Almost all of the land-based species included in this group fall into the family known as the *Testudinidae*.

PETS

Tortoises have been kept as pets for hundreds of years. Some of the larger species of Galapagos tortoises were brought back to the UK by Charles Darwin in 1836.

The first English 'tourists' to the Mediterranean, around the turn of the 20th century, were fond of returning with the tortoises they had found in that area. After the Second World War, the number of Mediterranean species imported into various countries steadily increased, reaching a peak in the 1960s and 1970s.

PRESERVATION

Such a massive raid on wild tortoises from the Mediterranean areas brought many species to the brink of extinction. In addition, many thousands died in transit or at their destinations, due to poor conditions and lack of knowledge about their needs.

This prompted the Convention on the International Trade of Endangered Species to consider

the Mediterranean species as animals at risk. In addition, some local governments placed their own bans on export, as Greece has done with the Marginated Tortoise. The import trade has, therefore, been practically halted.

This resulted in the pet industry turning its attention away from the Mediterranean species to more exotic, but less restricted, species such as the South American Tortoises, African Spurred and Leopard species. This has brought its own problems as these species have even more unique requirements, and many grow to unmanageable sizes.

Responsible tortoise ownership will help the conservation of the various species kept as pets.

INTERNATIONAL PROTECTION

Certain species of tortoise are included in the Convention on the International Trade of Endangered Species (CITES) lists as species which are threatened with extinction in their natural habitats.

As regards the tortoises mentioned in this book, the species thus affected are as follows:

The Spur-thighed Tortoise (*Testudo graeca*) (all subspecies thereof).

The Hermann's Tortoise (*Testudo hermanni*) (all subspecies thereof). The Marginated Tortoise (*Testudo marginata*).

Other species which are not included, such as the much rarer Egyptian Tortoise (*Testudo kleinmanni*) and the Pancake Tortoise (*Malacochersus tornieri*), also fall under these regulations.

In the majority of countries, the CITES regulations are enforced by local government law, therefore contacting the local government environment department is recommended to find out how each country enforces these rules.

The aim is to control strictly the sale of captive-bred species and to prevent the illegal import of wild tortoises for the pet trade.

Other tortoise species do not currently fall under such regulations, but this may well change in the near future as more wild species are threatened with depopulation.

OWNERSHIP

Tortoises make excellent pets. They are quiet, they do not need to be taken for long walks, and they are fascinating creatures to care for. There is always a reverse

Tortoises make excellent pets, as long as you are aware of their specific needs.

side to the coin, however, and the potential pet owner must consider the following.

- Depending on the species of tortoise kept, the requirements for housing will alter. Species from more tropical or equatorial regions do not hibernate during the winter. Consequently, they will require some form of indoor housing with heating and artificial ultraviolet lighting all year round.
- Some of the tropical species, such as the Red-Footed and Yellow-Footed Tortoises, enjoy soft fruits in their diets, whereas the Leopard and African Spurred Tortoises are more grass-grazing species, being used to the grasslands/savannahs of Africa. These dietary nuances can make the care of these tortoises more complicated and, indeed, more expensive.
- Finally, the long life-expectancy of most tortoises also has to be considered. "A tortoise is for the next century, not just for Christmas" is probably a fair comment!

THE SHELL

The tortoise and turtle families have evolved over millions of years. They look unlike any other land or aquatic animal, more closely resembling the beetle family in their design. The obvious and chief reason for this is their shell.

There are many popular misconceptions about turtle and tortoise shells. They are, in fact, made of living tissue. The main part of the shell is bone, complete with its own marrow cavity, covered in a layer of horny skin that provides the coloration and patterns seen on the individual species.

STRUCTURE

The shell is divided into a number of regions, all of which help to identify each species, and individuals within each species.

The upper shell is the carapace, and the lower or underside of the shell is the plastron. The carapace is attached to the plastron, between the front and rear limbs, by what are known as the pillars.

Finally, the individual carapace and plastron shells are divided into individual segments called scutes. These scutes are given names according to their positions on the body of the tortoise.

TRAUMA

The fact that the shell is alive has

important implications. Trauma to the shell can result in serious infections. Tortoises can also feel pain through injuries to their shells, and this has particular significance when restraining them. They should never be tethered to a rope or chain via a hole drilled in their shells, as was the practice a number of years ago.

RESPIRATION

There is only so much that a tortoise can fit inside its non-expanding shell. This can cause problems for the tortoise when breathing.

Other animals move their ribcage up and down to draw air in and out of the lungs, but tortoises cannot do this. They use their head, neck and limbs as bellows, moving them in and out of the shell, even during sleep, to push air in and out of the lungs.

A tortoise's lungs sit in the upper part of the shell, on top of the liver and digestive system. They do not have a true diaphragm to separate these functions so, if a tortoise is unfortunate enough to fall onto its back, its lungs become squashed under the weight of its gut. If the tortoise is not righted, this can lead to suffocation.

THE DIGESTIVE SYSTEM

The tortoise's digestive system is similar to that of many small herbivores such as guinea-pigs and

The digestive system is designed specifically for eating plant material.

rabbits in that it is supremely adapted to digesting plant material. It does this with the aid of microscopic bacteria and single-celled animals in its large intestine.

The digestive system empties into a common chamber with the kidneys and the reproductive system, which is known as the cloaca. This exits the body through the vent which is seen at the base of the underside of the tail. When a tortoise urinates, it often defecates as well. True faeces are the green or brown pellets passed.

THE URINARY SYSTEM

Tortoises produce a different form of urine from mammals. In mammals, urine waste (termed urea) is soluble. In reptiles and birds, much of the waste is not soluble, and is therefore termed uric acid. This is the white, cream or yellow portion of the faeces that tortoises pass. It is often accompanied by some more conventional watery urine.

Tortoises do have a bladder, but it works more as a water storage and absorption chamber and is not directly connected to the kidneys as it is in mammals. They can, however, suffer from bladder stones similar to those found in cats, dogs and humans.

THE REPRODUCTIVE SYSTEM

Tortoise reproductive organs are fully contained inside the shell in both sexes.

The female tortoise has two ovaries and a womb which empties into the cloaca.

The male has two testicles situated inside the shell near to the kidneys, and these empty the sperm via the *vas deferens* ducts, again directly into the cloaca.

In the male tortoise there is a phallus, but, unlike mammals, this has no part to play in urination. It is situated at rest in the base of the tail – hence males have longer tails than females in order to house this organ.

When mating occurs, the phallus becomes engorged with blood, everts through the vent, and forms a groove on its upper surface into which the sperm is deposited. It then penetrates the female tortoise's cloaca.

TEMPERATURE CONTROL

In common with all reptiles, tortoises are ectothermic, which means that they rely on their environment to provide their body heat. They are not like mammals, such as cats, dogs and humans, who can generate their own warmth.

A pet for life... the tortoise can live to over 100 years of age.

It is vitally important, for the health of the pet tortoise, that it is able to keep close to its Preferred Body Temperature (PBT). Therefore, the owner must provide the tortoise with an environment heated to its PBT range, either naturally by sunlight, or artificially with heaters.

This allows the tortoise to move from the cool to the hotter end of the range during the course of the day, to suit its needs at any given time.

Failure to provide enough heat will lead to poor immune system function, poor digestion, lethargy, poor appetite and, ultimately,

disease, stunted growth and, in severe cases, death. Too much heat will lead to dehydration, kidney damage and death.

LIFE-EXPECTANCY

This is a confusing area, as, theoretically, tortoises can live to well over 100 years of age if kept in the correct conditions, avoiding accidents. Many tortoises are considered juveniles up to the age of 10 years or so. Once past this age, they become sexually mature and can reproduce. Many continue to be able to reproduce right through their eighties and nineties!

2 *Tortoise Species*

The family *Testudinidae* is a moderate-sized one, comprising 41 living species.

Within this category are many well-known tortoises and many of these species have more than one name, depending on which country you are in or who you are speaking to.

As a result of this, the Latin names for tortoise species are normally used in books. This avoids confusion, but can be cumbersome. The list below is grouped according to Latin names for the species, but with some of their common name(s) given as well.

MEDITERRANEAN SPECIES

SPUR-THIGHED TORTOISE

As its name suggests, *Testudo graeca*, the Spur-Thighed Tortoise, has a conical piece of horny skin (the spur) on the back of each thigh. There is some diversity within this species, producing several subspecies. One of the subspecies is known as the Tunisian, North African or Mediterranean Spur-Thighed Tortoise *(Testudo graeca graeca)*.

This tortoise is found more in the south-western Mediterranean, along the North African coastline and Spain. It is a smaller tortoise, with a high-domed shell, and a dark underside. There is a large amount of yellow coloration over its head.

Spur-Thighed Tortoise: One of the smaller tortoises, with a high-domed shell.

Hermann's Tortoise: Its shell colour is dark yellow-green and black.

A similar subspecies is *Testudo graeca terrestris,* which is found in the Middle-East and is the smallest of the subspecies, although it has an even higher-domed shell. Both these subspecies prefer much hotter climates than the following two subspecies.

The first of these is the Asia Minor Spur-Thighed Tortoise *(Testudo graeca ibera),* found in the north-eastern Mediterranean around the Balkans, Greece and Turkey. It is the largest of the subspecies, with the shell reaching a length of 10 inches (25 cms) or more. The shell segments (scutes) are dotted with black spots on a yellow base, with a yellow hue to the head, neck and limbs.

Testudo graeca zarudnyi, the Iranian Spur-Thighed Tortoise, is the second largest of the subspecies. It is mainly a dark green to black colour, with a rounded upper shell (carapace) and dark-coloured legs. It is found in southern and eastern Iran. Both the Asia Minor and the Iranian Spur-Thighed Tortoises are capable of coping with more northerly climates.

There are two further recognised subspecies, *Testudo graeca anamurensis,* from the southern shores of Turkey, and *Testudo graeca nikolski,* from the northern shores of the Black Sea.

HERMANN'S TORTOISE

There are two subspecies recognised of *Testudo hermanni,* the Hermann's Tortoise. The Eastern Hermann's Tortoise *(Testudo hermanni boettgeri)* is found in the Balkans, Italy, Greece and Turkey. The Western Hermann's Tortoise *(Testudo hermanni hermanni)* is found in southern France, Spain, the Balearic Islands and Italy. These two subspecies are very similar in appearance. Their coloration is a dark yellow-green and black, and the species has no spur on the hind limbs. Fully grown, they can reach 9-10 inches (22-26 cms) in length and 4.5-5.5 lbs (2-2.5 kgs) in weight.

MARGINATED TORTOISE

Testudo marginata, the Marginated Tortoise, has a more restricted distribution than the Hermann's Tortoise, and is generally much less common in the wild and in captivity. It is found predominantly in the Greek mainland, from Mount Olympus to the Mediterranean coastline, as well as on the Greek islands. It has a yellow-green and black

Marginated Tortoise: This species can be difficult to keep in captivity.

coloration, and is distinguished by its undulating shell margin, which flares outwards towards the rear. Some individuals may have small horny spurs on their thighs. It is much more susceptible to disease than other Mediterranean species because of its specialised habitat requirements, often poorly replicated in captivity.

HORSFIELD'S TORTOISE

Testudo horsfieldi, the Horsfield's Tortoise, has also been referred to as the Russian, Steppe, Iranian, or Turkish Tortoise. It is found at the eastern end of the Mediterranean, around the Black and Caspian Seas right through to Afghanistan, and is, therefore, one of the more northerly tortoises. Despite this, it still prefers dry, rocky terrain close to streams where herbage is present. It is a yellow-green colour, with a very dark underside to its slightly flattened shell. The species has four claws only on each forelimb, unlike the other three Mediterranean species which have five. It tends to be slightly smaller than the Hermann's and Asia Minor Spur-Thighed species.

Most Horsfield's have a horny scale forming a point on the tip of the tail, and some possess small horny spurs on their thighs,

Horsfield's Tortoise: A northernly species which can tolerate cooler temperatures.

similar to the Spur-Thighed Tortoise. This species can better withstand cooler climates due to its more northerly habitat and the fact that it is found at relatively high altitudes over 4-5,000 feet. In the wild, this species also hibernates, burrowing into the soil to escape the frosts which occur during the winter, and also to escape from the heat of the day. In captivity, this species makes an excellent burrower, escape artist and lawn ruiner!

The Horsfield's Tortoise has a very short period of activity in the wild, lasting three months from April/May to August. Indeed, during the peak of the summer heat when temperatures exceed 86 degrees Fahrenheit (30 degrees Celsius), this tortoise may go into a period of near-hibernation (known as aestivation) in its burrow. A problem, when considering keeping Horsfield's Tortoises in captivity with more exotic, warmth-loving tortoises, is the fact that the former must be kept relatively dry, as dampness leads to shell infections more commonly than in other Mediterranean species.

NON-MEDITERRANEAN SPECIES

In the past, nearly all pet tortoises came from the Mediterranean. However, the non-Mediterranean species are now becoming much more popular.

LEOPARD TORTOISE

There are two subspecies of *Geochelone pardalis,* the Leopard Tortoise. The first, the Western Leopard Tortoise *(Geochelone pardalis pardalis)* is found in South Africa, while the second, the Eastern Leopard Tortoise *(Geochelone pardalis babcocki)* is found in East Africa down to eastern parts of South Africa.

The Leopard Tortoise is, as its name suggests, beautifully marked, with a yellow shell covered in black spots and stars. The shell may be raised in multiple small domes, a feature which appears in this species and other related ones such as the Indian Starred Tortoise. The Leopard Tortoise will grow considerably more than the Mediterranean species and may attain weights of 66-88 lbs (30-40 kgs) when fully grown, although 22-33 lbs (10-15 kgs) is more common.

Specialist vivaria are required for overwintering this species, particularly if they are kept in colder northerly climates, as the Leopard Tortoise loves heat and does not hibernate. It also enjoys roaming, so large enclosures, or even heated greenhouses, make better accommodation than tank-like vivaria.

AFRICAN SPURRED TORTOISE

Geochelone sulcata, the African Spurred Tortoise, is found in the Sudan and on the central African savannahs. Like the Leopard Tortoise, this is chiefly a grass-grazing tortoise that requires high environmental temperatures, necessitating specialist vivaria and heating equipment to keep it

Leopard Tortoise: This species has a yellow shell covered in black spots and stars.

17

African Spurred Tortoise: The largest mainland tortoise, this species needs spacious accommodation and a warm environment.

properly in northerly climates.

It is the largest mainland tortoise (only the tortoises of the Galapagos and Seychelles islands being larger), reaching lengths of 24-31 inches (60-80 cms) and weights in excess of 176 lbs (80 kgs) in the wild!

This poses a problem with housing. Outdoor pens or greenhouses are required to keep them warm throughout the year as this species does not hibernate.

INDIAN STARRED TORTOISE

Geochelone elegans, the Indian Starred Tortoise, is another beautifully marked tortoise with a cream-yellow shell with dark star-shaped patterns on each segment. The head is cream-coloured with black spots. The female, like the Leopard Tortoise, has more curved and longer hind-limb claws to allow for nest-building.

Their habitat in the wild covers most of India, south-east Pakistan and Sri Lanka. This has created some regional variation, although at the moment no specific subspecies have been recognised. Those from Pakistan and northern India are darker brown in colour, whereas the more southerly mainland types are smaller and have a creamier background with dark spots.

The Sri Lanka Starred Tortoises are the same size as the ones from Pakistan, but have the markings of those from the southern mainland. They are slightly larger than the Mediterranean species, but do not get much beyond 11-15 lbs (5-7

Indian Star Tortoise: This spectacularly marked tortoise has a star-shaped pattern on each segment of its shell.

kgs) in weight and 10 inches (25 cms) in length.

Their upper shells (carapace) may exhibit some 'bumps' rather than the smooth shell expected of the Mediterranean species. This feature may be inherited as not all Starred Tortoises show it. Specialist vivaria are required for this species to maintain environmental temperatures as near to its natural habitat as possible.

CHACO TORTOISE

Geochelone chilensis, the Chaco Tortoise, is found in central South America from Argentina through to Venezuela and Paraguay.

It is smaller than its cousins, the Red-Footed and Yellow-Footed Tortoises (also known as Red-Legged and Yellow-Legged Tortoises), being on average 7-10 inches (18-25 cms) in length. Its shell is less domed, and has a serrated rim. Its colour is a yellow-beige with relatively few markings. Some Chacos exhibit spurs or several prominent scales on the back of their thighs.

In its natural habitat, the Chaco inhabits open grasslands and deciduous woodlands. Due to its preference for warm climates, it needs to be kept in a purpose-built vivarium in the UK and other northerly areas. In such areas, the Chaco may live outside during the warmer summers, but will need to be brought inside as and when the weather changes. This species will become less active during the winter, although they do not hibernate and must still have supplemental heating all year round.

RED-FOOTED TORTOISE

Geochelone carbonaria is known as the Red-Footed Tortoise, the Red-Foot Tortoise, or the Baby Red-Footed Tortoise.

It has a dark-brown to black shell, with brown or yellow spots in the middle of each of the shell segments. Its underside is yellowish with black spots, and it has pink-red and yellow scales over its legs and head. Individuals may also appear to have a 'waist' or narrowing of the shell in front of the hind limbs.

It is found in South America, deep in the tropical rainforests on both sides of the Andes, as well as on some Caribbean islands.

Males can grow to 12-20 inches (30-50 cms) long and weigh 22-33 lbs (10-15 kgs). They tend to

Red-Footed Tortoise: A native of the South American tropical rainforest, the Red-Footed Tortoise does not hibernate.

have a slightly dished or concave underside (plastron) to the shell. Females tend to be slightly smaller at 10-20 inches (25-40 cms).

Due to its tropical rainforest habitat, this species does not hibernate and needs indoor specialist vivaria to keep it at the correct temperatures and humidity all year round.

During hot summers they can be allowed into outdoor pens. There is some evidence that a smaller variation of the Red-Footed Tortoise exists, which looks the same but reaches only 6-8 inches (15-20 cms) in length.

YELLOW-FOOTED TORTOISE

Geochelone denticulata, the Yellow-Footed Tortoise also known as the Forest Tortoise, also derives from the South American rainforests east of the Andes. As its name suggests, it has yellow scales over its head and limbs, but it otherwise resembles the Red-Footed Tortoise in many respects, although it does not have a 'waist'. It is slightly larger than the Red-Footed Tortoise, reaching 18-24 inches (45-60 cms) in length.

Due to this species' tropical background, specialist vivaria and indoor all-year-round heating are required.

Like the Red-Footed Tortoise, it requires high temperature and humidity levels in captivity, unlike many other tortoises which enjoy heat, but prefer more arid conditions. Again like the Red-Footed Tortoise, the Yellow-Footed Tortoise enjoys fruit as well as green foods.

3 *Choosing Your Tortoise*

Owning a tortoise is a great responsibility, as is the care of any living creature. In the case of many tortoise species, their numbers in the wild are dwindling.

The entire *Testudinidae* ('true tortoise' family) is listed by the Convention on International Trade in Endangered Species (CITES). This is the worldwide organisation responsible for regulating endangered animals and plants, either as species threatened with extinction, or species which will shortly become threatened unless trade in them is regulated and restricted.

RESPONSIBILITY

Before buying a tortoise, you must ask yourself several questions.
- Do you understand the care which will be needed for the particular species of tortoise you purchase?
- Can you provide the housing

Think very carefully before taking on the responsibility of owning a tortoise.

and, if necessary, the heating and lighting required? Even for Mediterranean species, heating may be needed, considering the poorer summers experienced in the cooler climates of Northern Europe and the USA.

- Do you realise that some tortoises may become ill, which will possibly necessitate the prevention of hibernation by keeping them warm and active during the winter months?
- Can you care for the sick tortoise? Hopefully, this will not happen, but even the best-kept tortoises can fall prey to a number of diseases.
- When this happens, it is necessary to seek the services of a vet who knows about reptiles. Medical care can sometimes be expensive, particularly as tortoises tend to become ill slowly and hence recovery is equally slow! Are you prepared for this expense?

VENDORS

Tortoises are best purchased from reputable breeders who are often, by the very nature of their enthusiasm for the species, not professional retailers.

Finding these breeders can be difficult, but this should not put off the responsible potential owner. The alternative is the purchase of tortoises from less reliable commercial sources, where there is the possibility that the tortoises being sold may be wild-caught rather than captive-bred. This is a very important point to consider.

Captive-bred individuals are the ideal tortoise for the enthusiast. They are already acclimatised to captivity, they are frequently bred by caring individuals who will pay attention to potential hazards such as parasites, and they do not threaten the wild population further.

Wild-caught tortoises are the prime reason for the endangered state of the species. They are extremely highly stressed individuals by the time they reach the shores of the importing country, and often heavily parasitised with worms and other organisms which will weaken them further.

The tortoises are then placed into vivaria tanks, a considerable change from the savannahs of Africa, or the rocky coastlines of the Mediterranean and, by the time a potential owner purchases them, they are a medical disaster waiting to happen!

Reputable breeders may be found by contacting your local reptile/herpetological society, your local reptile vet, or through one of the very worthwhile tortoise/reptile organisations which exist in many countries.

WHAT SPECIES?

Choice may well be restricted by what species are available, but careful thought needs to go into making your decision.

Do you want to go for the more northerly and generally hardier tortoise, such as the Mediterranean species, or the more exotic tropical and equatorial species? There are pros and cons involved with them all.

MEDITERRANEAN

The Mediterranean species may well withstand the cooler summers of Northern Europe and the USA better and, conveniently, will hibernate through the worst of the winter months. The Horsfield's Tortoise is particularly durable, owing to its more northerly natural habitat, although it detests wet conditions, which increase the chances of shell infections.

However, there are species within this group which are less well suited. The Marginated

The Horsfield's Tortoise is an excellent choice, as it tends to be more hardy.

Tortoise, for example, is increasingly rarely found in captivity as it is much less tolerant of cold summers and more prone to a number of tortoise diseases than the hardier Hermann's or Spur-Thighed species.

In addition, there are subspecies of the Spur-Thighed group, such as the Tunisian Spur-Thighed Tortoise, which prefer warmer summers than the Asia Minor Spur-Thighed Tortoise, and who only hibernate for very short periods, much shorter than the cold northerly winters.

This means that some form of supplemental in-house vivarium will be required, with heating and artificial ultraviolet lighting for part of the year.

The Mediterranean species should be supplied with a hide box if left in a garden during the summer, so they can get away from potential predators such as foxes, particularly at night.

Is your garden tortoise-proof or can a pet tortoise escape? It is worth noting that some species such as the Horsfield's Tortoise can burrow under fences, and the majority of species can climb over steps and barricades which are equal to or less than their length. In addition, of course, provision of an area for hibernation is needed, come the winter.

Some of the advantages of the Mediterranean breeds are not only that they are more used to northerly climates, but they rarely grow excessively large. A fully-grown adult Hermann's or Spur-Thighed Tortoise will be around 25-30 centimetres (10-12 inches) in length and weigh from 2.2-2.6 kilograms (5-6 lbs). This makes them easier to manage than the more exotic non-Mediterranean species.

NON-MEDITERRANEAN

The non-Mediterranean species can be equally problematic. As a rule, they will all need a purpose-built tank or vivarium, as they do not hibernate in the winter, and will need higher environmental temperatures all the year round. These equate to 25-35°C (77-95°F) temperature ranges as opposed to 20-27°C (68-77°F) for the Mediterranean species.

This does not mean that they cannot be allowed out in the garden during the hotter summer days. Indeed for the African Spurred and Leopard Tortoises, as well as to a lesser extent the Indian Starred Tortoise, this is to be encouraged as they will graze on large quantities of grasses in their native habitats.

This is in addition to the exposure of the tortoise to ultraviolet light, an essential for any species. Like humans, they require this to synthesise vitamin D3, which is needed to enable normal bone and shell development. It is, perhaps, more important for the larger and more rapidly growing breeds such as the Leopard, African Spurred and Indian Starred Tortoises.

For the rest of the year, when it may be too cold outside for these more tropical species, an in-tank heating system is needed along with an in-tank ultraviolet lighting system. This becomes less essential in much older tortoises, but in

A tropical species, such as the Indian Star Tortoise, can be allowed in the garden on hot, summer days.

younger growing species (which roughly applies to the first 10-15 years of their lives), lack of ultraviolet light exposure, particularly combined with a lack of dietary calcium, causes terrible shell and limb deformities similar to rickets in humans.

Other special requirements apply to the tropical species such as the Yellow- and Red-Footed and Chaco Tortoises from South America. These species require high humidity in their tanks as well as year-round high environmental temperatures. This will demand that the owner sprays the inside of the tank with a water mister several times a day, as the higher vivarium temperatures rapidly dry out the tank and air.

EXOTIC

Of the more exotic species, the Leopard Tortoise is gaining popularity, as it tends to be more robust and less prone to problems

in captivity, whereas the rarer Indian Starred Tortoise requires more privacy and can be challenging to keep in a more northerly clime.

The Red- and Yellow-Footed Tortoises are also less robust and require more care and attention, and so are not so suited to the novice tortoise keeper. You also have to consider the size these species will grow to. The Leopard Tortoise in its native Africa may exceed 40 kilograms in weight (the weight of a Rottweiler!) and the African Spurred Tortoise can double that, this being the largest mainland tortoise!

The Red-Footed Tortoise may well grow up to 50 centimetres (20 inches) in length and weigh tens of kilograms in the process, with the Yellow-Footed Tortoise slightly exceeding this.

Enclosures which start out as large tank vivaria may rapidly have to extend to outhouses or rooms dedicated to the care of these species! Outdoor enclosures are, therefore, often needed, and require to be equipped with heating and ultraviolet lighting. It is worth noting that the African Spurred Tortoise, like the Mediterranean Horsfield's, is an excellent digger, reducing enclosures and gardens to lunar landscapes relatively easily.

MALE OR FEMALE?

This can be a difficult question to answer.

Female tortoises when sexually mature (generally from 7-8 years of age depending on the individual species) may start to lay infertile eggs, like domestic chickens, even when there are no other tortoises present. This can lead to medical problems, such as egg-binding, whereby eggs become stuck in the tortoise's reproductive tract, or to a condition known as pre-ovulatory stasis. This is where the ovaries fail to shed their eggs into the reproductive tract, and so swell up, decreasing the space inside the tortoise's shell available for the gut or lungs. These emergencies frequently necessitate surgery, and consequently carry a risk to the animal's life. Males obviously tend

to be less prone to reproductive problems, although their risk of other medical diseases is much the same.

In general, males tend to be slightly more aggressive to other tortoises and to other pets. Females seem to be more tractable.

SEXING

Determining the sex of a tortoise is fraught with difficulties. This is often because owners try and discover this before the tortoise is sexually mature (i.e. before 7-8 years of age) and hence many of the secondary sexual characteristics have not yet developed. When purchasing a hatchling tortoise, it is not possible to be accurate about its sex.

• Males have a longer tail than females, as the male phallus is housed in the tail region. When viewed from the underside, the vent (the common opening of the digestive, reproductive and urinary systems) is often beyond the margin of the upper shell (or carapace as it is known), whereas, with female tortoises, the vent is within the carapace margin.
• Males will often have a slightly

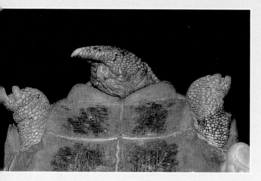 

The male's tail (left) is longer than the female's tail (right).

The male (left) has a slightly dished underside. The female (right) has a flatter underside.

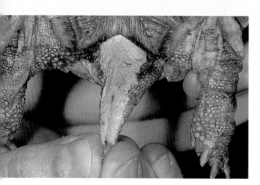 

The male vent (left) has a deeper, V-shaped anal notch. The female's vent (right) is shallower to aid egg-laying.

dished underside (known as the plastron) to their shell, which complements the domed carapace of the female tortoise, allowing easier mating to occur. In females the plastron is flatter.

- Males of some species, such as the Indian Starred Tortoise, are considerably smaller than the females when fully grown. However, in other species such as the Red-Footed Tortoise, the male is larger than the female.
- Some males may have an obvious hook to the end of the tail, as in Horsfield's Tortoise.
- The female Leopard Tortoise and the Indian Starred Tortoise have elongated hind-limb claws, thought to improve their digging abilities when egg-laying.
- Males will often have a deeper V-shaped anal notch to the end of the plastron to allow the phallus to exit the tail, whereas the notch in females is shallower, thus aiding egg-laying.
- Females in some Mediterranean species, such as the Hermann's or Spur-Thighed Tortoises, may have a hinge joint to the plastron. This occurs towards the rear of the plastron to allow it to deflect downwards and increase the width of the gap between carapace and plastron near the tail, so making the laying of eggs easier.

NUMBERS

Should you have more than one tortoise? To a certain extent this will depend on space, as well as finance. Tortoises are often solitary creatures in the wild, although hatchlings (very young tortoises) seem to appreciate company.

MIXING SEXES

It is important that males and females are not kept in close proximity unless it is intended that they should breed. This is because males, during the breeding season, will continually harass any females in their territory, which can lead to unacceptable levels of stress for the female tortoises.

Males may also fight with each other over a female, leading to shell damage. Males kept in a large enough enclosure without females can still fight; females kept without males are more tolerant.

MIXING SPECIES

Mixed species exhibits can be set up but care should be taken when mixing species with different housing requirements. For example, Red-Footed Tortoises have a totally different vivarium requirement to Leopard Tortoises, the former needing much higher humidity, as well as different food types. In addition, the mixing of giant species, such as the African Spurred, or Leopard Tortoises with small Mediterranean species such as the Tunisian Spur-Thighed Tortoise is not to be recommended.

Another problem with species interaction is disease. Some species such as the Marginated Tortoise are extremely susceptible to upper respiratory tract diseases such as the herpes virus infection which is part of the 'runny nose syndrome' of tortoises. This infection may be carried and passed on by other species of tortoise without showing signs of disease, but the Marginated Tortoise, if exposed to it, will invariably develop the disease which can prove fatal.

CHILDREN

In general, tortoises do not make good children's pets, for a number of reasons. One is the high level of care which needs to be provided for tortoises, day in and day out, for the duration of their hopefully long lives. This is taxing enough for an adult, but frequently escapes children.

Children can enjoy tortoises, but the responsibility of care must rest with an adult.

Another very important point to consider is the potential for reptiles of any shape or form to pass dangerous bacterial infections on to human handlers. Tortoises are no exception to this, and perfectly healthy tortoises may carry species of the bacteria *Salmonella*, as well as E. coli subtypes, and many other food poisoning bacteria, in their digestive systems without any obvious signs of disease.

Transmission occurs after handling the tortoise, or its faeces, and then placing contaminated hands into the mouth. It cannot occur via the unbroken skin, but it is possible to develop unpleasant skin infections from open wounds exposed to this.

PETS

It is worthwhile considering the role of other household pets when deciding on purchasing a tortoise.

- Many dogs, for example, will 'worry' tortoises. They can cause severe trauma to limbs, head and neck and the shell. If the species is small enough, or the tortoise young enough, then a dog may be able to pick it up and drop it, fracturing the shell.

- Other pets, such as cats and ferrets, should be considered as potential threats to a tortoise's wellbeing, as neither family of animals is above taking the odd swipe at a strange intruder on their territory.

CARRIERS

When your pet tortoise is transported, it is important that the correct equipment is used. In general, commercial cat-carriers fit the requirements well.

- Tortoises can be potentially very heavy for their size, so make sure the container is strong enough to support the tortoise's weight.

- Your tortoise can slide about inside the container. To

A cat should always be considered as a potential threat to a tortoise.

minimise this, pad the container well with straw or hay, or even shredded paper, which will also keep the tortoise thermally insulated when being transported in cooler weather. Indeed, it may be advisable to use a hot-water bottle wrapped in a towel in the bottom of the container, if a long journey is planned in the winter with a non-hibernating tortoise.

HANDLING

Tortoises are wriggly at the best of times and can manoeuvre their front and hind limbs, most of which have very sharp claws, into position to scratch the hands holding them. Tortoises are also surprisingly strong. These two factors can easily cause them to break free from an owner's grasp and risk being dropped. It is best to hold the tortoise with both hands from either side at the midpoint of the shell between fore and hind limbs. Larger species may require more than one handler.

The correct way to handle a tortoise.

4 *Tortoise Accommodation*

The accommodation required for your pet tortoise will depend on its species.

Tortoises from tropical and equatorial regions have more specialised requirements than the Mediterranean types, which are slightly less demanding.

MEDITERRANEAN SPECIES

OUTDOOR SHELTERS

If the weather and your circumstances permit it, then allowing these species into an enclosed and secure garden during the warmer summer months is advised.

The freedom to roam, combined with access to unfiltered natural sunlight, has a positive effect on the health of any tortoise.

However, it is essential that the environmental temperatures do not drop below 16-18°C (60.8-64.4°F) or 20-24°C (68-75.2°F, for juvenile tortoises).

Security

If you are providing outdoor accommodation, the garden must be secure. Most tortoises can dig, and the Horsfield's is an expert burrower, so some thought must be given to providing subterranean fencing, similar to rabbit-proof fencing.

The Hide

It is advisable to have a hide for the tortoises to retreat to in bad weather, and in which to escape from predators such as foxes if they are routinely being left outside overnight.

These constructions can be made from marine plyboard which makes them waterproof, with a mono-angled roof covered in roofing felt, like a garden shed. Basically, a hide is a rectangular box.

• The height should be slightly more than the height of the

A hide fitted with a ramp. This provides an easy retreat in bad weather.

largest tortoise's carapace, for which it is to act as accommodation. Tortoises do not seem to like extremely tall hides, and this configuration also minimises volume and, consequently, heat loss.

- The area of the box should not be too large, as the idea is that this should be a cosy night roost for the tortoises and not a permanent pen. Therefore, providing the floor space is 2-3 times the area covered by the tortoises themselves, they will be able to retain heat, and the feeling of security can be enhanced.
- The whole shelter may be raised on low legs, so reducing the dampness within the construction.
- Access to the shelter can be via a shallow ramp, with the entrance covered with heavy-duty clear polyurethane stapled to the door lintel, providing protection from the wind and rain.
- The inside of the shelter may then be bedded with straw, hay or torn up newspaper.
- For additional warmth in more northerly climes, you can use a radiating heat mat. This will need to be wired to an out-of-doors circuit and circuit breaker system, placed underneath the shelter and insulated in order to trap heat upwards into the shelter. Most commercial outlets catering for reptiles will sell these radiating heat mats, and garden centres or electrical stores can give advice on electrical connectors which are safe to use outside.

INDOOR HOUSING

For those who live in more northerly climes, where the summers are not reliable, serious consideration is needed for vivaria equipment in which to house the pet tortoise during the cooler weather.

Even in warm climates, it may still be necessary for medical reasons to prevent a Mediterranean tortoise from hibernating, and therefore some form of artificial heating and lighting system will be required.

Vivaria

The traditional vivarium is often an adapted glass or perspex fish tank. These are not ideal for tortoises as the dimensions are all geared towards height rather than floor area, and tortoises, as one would expect, are not best adapted to exploring vertical space!

Space

The minimum requirement for floor space of any system should be four times the area of the total number of tortoises kept.

Heating

Two forms of heaters are recommended. A heater is required to provide continuous background heat. This is best provided by a radiating heat mat

A vivarium can be fitted out to provide suitable indoor accommodation.

which is placed on the *outside* of the glass or perspex tank.

As its name suggests, it radiates heat through the tank wall, and so does not require to be in direct contact with the tortoise, which is an asset as far as hygiene and safety are concerned.

The size of this mat depends on the volume of the tank, but it should be roughly one-third to one-half the size of the largest side of the tank.

In addition, a basking, or hot-spot-producing, heater is required to provide the real heat beloved of many tortoises. Suspend a ceramic bulb heater from the roof of the tank, ensuring that it is well out of reach of the tortoise!

Any commercial reptile outlet can supply these, but they should be attached to the mains electricity via a thermostat device so that you can set the temperature to the required level.

For most Mediterranean tortoises the basking area should reach 32-34°C (89.6-93.2°F). This temperature should decline from the area of the heat lamp, to reach a cooler temperature of 20-24°C (68-75.2°F) at the other end of the tank. The tortoise therefore has a choice, and can move itself during the day, so regulating its own body temperature.

During the night, the environmental temperature may be dropped by 4-5°C, (39.2-41°F) but the coolest end of the tank should not dip below 18°C (64.4°F).

Lighting
Tank lighting is also important, particularly for juvenile growing tortoises which have a high requirement for vitamin D3 for bone growth. This is manufactured in the tortoise's skin under the influence of ultraviolet light, particularly the B part of the spectrum.

To prevent growth deformities in the bones, and to act as a general appetite stimulant, the tortoise needs to be provided with an ultraviolet light which provides these UV-B rays. Natural sunlight cannot provide this for indoor tortoises as these rays are filtered out by glass, and hence any UV lighting must be on the *inside* of the tank.

Most reptile commercial outlets will supply the strip lights which are safe for tortoises and power packs to run them. The light should be positioned so that it is within 30-40 centimetres (12-15 inches) of the tortoises at all

The Red-Footed tortoise needs a specialist indoor vivaria to provide the correct heat and humidity.

times, as the UV rays diminish rapidly with distance.

The lighting should be kept on for 12-14 hours per day during the summer or, if you are trying to prevent hibernation, it should mimic the longer summer days.

Substrates

The floor covering should keep the cage free from moisture, as most of the Mediterranean species prefer dry conditions. You can use an inexpensive material such as newspaper, which is clean to use, and it is easy to see when it becomes dirty, so cage hygiene is preserved.

Alternatively, sand may be used for the Mediterranean species, although there is some risk of the tortoise consuming the sand and getting a gut blockage over time. Other options include the use of hay or straw, or one of the commercial synthetic grass carpets which are sold in many reptile shops. These are more difficult to keep clean, and to see when they become dirty, so vigilance is necessary.

Furniture

Many tortoises appreciate a 'hide' within the tank. This can be made of marine plyboard or even stiff cardboard and should be just high enough to permit entry, and of an area roughly twice that of the total area covered by all the tortoises present.

It should be sited at the cooler end of the tank away from the hot-spot basking lamp, as tortoises in the wild will seek this sort of shelter to get away from the midday glare of the sun.

NON-MEDITERRANEAN SPECIES

These species all come from warmer climates than the Mediterranean species, and so can only be kept outside for any length of the time in southern Europe, Australia and the southern states of the USA, or in their native homes.

Otherwise, in the UK and northern USA for example, they may only be housed outside during the warmest parts of the summer if provided with appropriate heated shelters for overnight accommodation.

OUTDOORS

Some of these animals can become extremely large, for example the Leopard and African Spurred Tortoises, so garden fences need to be made of steel posts and heavy stock fencing, or solid wooden fencing.

It is important that the barrier provided is not a transparent one, such as uncovered wire mesh. This is because tortoises will patrol the perimeter fences of any enclosure and have a habit of trying to walk through such 'see-through' obstacles. The fencing may have to be extended 30-60 centimetres below ground for the containment of species such as the African Spurred Tortoise, which is a prodigious digger.

Shelters

Any penned area should provide some shelter, both in the form of obstacles such as plants (making sure they are not poisonous), logs and rocks to escape from the heat than one tortoise is kept together, and a hutch-like shelter for protection and warmth overnight.

The construction of such a

An outdoor shelter should include a hide, and a securely penned grazing area.

shelter is much as described above for Mediterranean species, the major difference being that, in the UK and northern USA, some form of heating is almost always required. This can be provided by a radiant heat mat, as previously mentioned, attached to an outside circuit system.

Temperature

Attention should be paid to the temperatures required by these species, as they must not be allowed outside if night-time, or daytime temperatures are below 18°C (64.4°F). This, then, is the minimum temperature aimed for in the tortoise shelter.

Preferably, the hottest part of the day should be in the region of 24-25°C (75.2-77°F) and above for these more tropical species.

Kennels

For larger adults such as the Leopard and African Spurred Tortoises, consideration needs to be given to building purpose-designed outdoor kennels and pens.

These may be adapted from garden sheds or reinforced greenhouses, or they may be built along the lines of large dog kennels with a paddock area.

The advantage of this system is that a proper heating arrangement can be installed in the housing area, with a ceramic bulb heater which is thermostatically controlled to ensure the proper temperatures are adhered to.

The height of the 'kennel' must therefore allow the tortoise access and then leave some space to suspend the heating lamp or lamps.

If these are to be the tortoises' permanent residences, then the minimum floor area should be four times the area covered by all of the tortoises sharing the accommodation.

Paddocks

The attached paddock area for the larger Leopard and African Spurred Tortoises may need to be of a size in the order of 10-12 metres (33-39.6 ft) squared per tortoise, a not inconsiderable space!

The South American tortoises (the Red- and Yellow-Footed and Chaco) all have a higher requirement for environmental humidity as they come from a rainforest-style habitat. Their paddocks must therefore provide more vegetation and herbage, whereas the Leopard, Starred and

African Spurred Tortoises can cope with open grassland with the odd piece of shelter.

Indeed these two species, being from a savannah-style habitat, thrive on open grassland, and become frustrated when they cannot exercise on a daily basis.

INDOOR HOUSING

The requirements are basically similar to that provided for the Mediterranean species. There are one or two differences.

Lighting

The larger species such as the Indian Starred, Leopard and African Spurred Tortoises all grow relatively quickly, and so have a higher requirement for ultraviolet light than the slower-growing Mediterranean species. The provision of a good-quality ultraviolet light, and the exposure of these tortoises to unfiltered natural sunlight (weather permitting) is essential.

These larger species may also outgrow any indoor accommodation an owner can provide, short of setting aside a room for them! This may necessitate the building of an

If you are keeping more than one tortoise, you must make sure there is enough room for both to live happily in the vivarium.

outside shelter/shed/kennel and providing heating and lighting there, as mentioned above.

Temperature

Temperature requirements are also higher than for the Mediterranean species. Most require a hot spot area providing temperatures of 34-36°C (93.2-95°F) and giving an overall average tank day-time temperature of 26-28°C (78.8-82.4°F) with a night-time average temperature of 20-22°C (68-71.6°F). The Red-Footed and the Chaco tortoises are slightly hardier, but the Indian Starred Tortoise can become susceptible to medical problems if kept below this temperature range.

Humidity

Another factor to consider is the humidity. The African species such as the Leopard and African Spurred Tortoises as well as the Indian Starred Tortoise, prefer drier climates. It is important to provide them with water for drinking, and to bathe them every now and then in tepid water to encourage drinking, but their tank should be dry.

Substrate

The use of sand, newspaper or straw as bedding and covering for the floor of the tank is recommended. For the South American species, particularly the Yellow-Footed Tortoise, the tank needs to be kept relatively humid. This requires misting the tank with previously boiled and cooled water by means of a plant sprayer several times a day in order to keep the humidity above 50-60 per cent. For this reason, the use of a substrate which holds more water, such as damp peat moss or alfalfa/rabbit grass pellets, is useful.

Hides

Each tank should have a hide area for privacy, and as a retreat when it becomes too hot. Therefore, as with the Mediterranean species, the hide should be placed at the other end of the tank from the basking lamp.

5 *General Care*

There are three particular areas which require special attention in order to ensure your tortoise's general health and wellbeing. You need to care for the tortoise's shell, to appreciate the full cycle involved in hibernation, and also to understand the tortoise's behaviour patterns.

SHELL CARE
DEHYDRATION

Pay particular attention to a tortoise's fluid consumption, as there is, currently, a fair amount of evidence that many captive tortoises become chronically dehydrated during the course of their lives, which can cause progressive kidney damage. A method of encouraging tortoises to drink, as well as cleaning the shell and hydrating their skin, is to bathe them in lukewarm water. Many species enjoy this, particularly the South American and Leopard Tortoises.

BATHING

The bathing process should be performed once weekly for the Mediterranean, Indian and African species which are more used to arid conditions.

You can bath as often as every second or third day for the humidity-loving South American species.

Your tortoise will enjoy a regular, weekly bath, but keep a close check on the shell at all times.

Put the tortoise into a shallow container. Add previously boiled and then cooled water to a depth which laps on the upper surface of the plastron (usually 2-5 centimetres/1-2 inches depth).

Scoop water over the tortoise's carapace. The tortoise should be left for 15-20 minutes so that the skin can absorb the water and the tortoise can drink it.

Remember that tortoises have no hard palate separating their nasal passages from their mouth. To create enough suction to enable them to drink, they must submerge their nostrils in the water as well as their mouths, which means that the water must be several centimetres deep.

The Horsfield's Tortoise may hibernate for five to six months in its native habitat.

the shell and reaching the pale-coloured living bone underneath should immediately be brought to the attention of a reptile vet, as deep shell infections, once started, can be difficult to treat and may cause life-threatening septicaemia.

HIBERNATION

Only the Mediterranean tortoises truly hibernate during the winter. Even then, there is some variation, with the Middle Eastern and Tunisian subspecies of Spur-Thighed Tortoise hibernating in the wild for 2-3 months at most, whereas the Horsfield's Tortoise may hibernate for 5-6 months in its native habitat.

ENVIRONMENT

- Remove any abrasive floor surfaces, such as uncovered concrete, which could traumatise the plastron.
- Prevent persistently damp conditions for species such as the Horsfield's Tortoise which comes from an arid climate, otherwise these will lead to fungal and bacterial infections of the shell (known colloquially as shell rot).
- Any trauma penetrating the coloured outer horny layer of

WHY HIBERNATE?
Reasons For:

- It sets up the reproductive system of both sexes to allow egg production in the females and mating behaviour in the males the following spring.

- There is some evidence that hibernation allows the tortoise to live longer by allowing normal thyroid function (the gland which controls an animal's metabolism).
- The tortoise obviously stops feeding during hibernation, at a time when temperatures are naturally colder and daylight shorter. Preventing hibernation requires the owner to fool the tortoise into thinking it is still summer with artificial lighting and heat, just to keep it eating.

  This can be fraught with problems, and many overwintered unhibernated Mediterranean species will become anorexic.

Against:
- No tortoise which is underweight, or suffering from some form of disease, should be allowed to go into hibernation, as healthy tortoises will lose up to 5-6 per cent of their body weight during this period.
- The tortoise's immune system is much less active. If a tortoise is suffering from some form of infectious disease, or parasites such as worms, these can multiply almost unchallenged during this period.

HEALTH CHECKS
A Mediterranean tortoise must be thoroughly checked over to ensure it is free of any disease one to two months prior to hibernation in October and November. This should be performed by a knowledgeable vet.

One of the basic measurements which can be performed on a Mediterranean tortoise prior to it going into hibernation, is to measure its body/plastron length in millimetres, compare this with its weight in grams, and plot against a graph of known normal values. This graph is known as the Jackson's Ratio graph.

Any Mediterranean tortoise falling significantly below the average weight against length line should be prevented from hibernating that year.

PREPARATION
If the tortoise in question is healthy enough to consider hibernation, then the following steps can be taken:-

- Feed carbohydrate-rich foods for the last 4-6 weeks or so before hibernation, i.e. from September. Examples are steamed pumpkin, carrots or swede, alfalfa pellets, mixed

JACKSON'S RATIO GRAPH

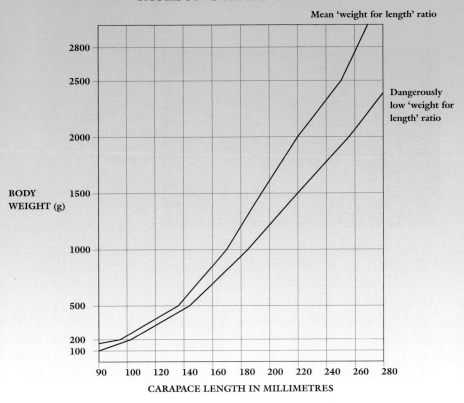

Reproduced from the BSAVA Manual of Exotic Pets, 3rd edition, edited by Peter H Beynon and John E Cooper (1991) with permission of BSAVA.

fruits such as melon, papaya, mango, figs, apples etc.

- As hibernation approaches and the daylight length reduces (if providing indoor ultraviolet lighting this must be done manually, reducing the light exposure from 12-14 hours to 8-9 hours), the tortoise's appetite will dwindle. Food should be withheld totally for the last 7-10 days before hibernation. During this time water should be provided and the temperature kept around 18-22°C (64-71°F). The tortoise will be active, and will continue to drink and defecate, emptying its digestive system of food which could ferment dangerously during the hibernation period.

- After this 7-10 day starvation period, the tortoise should be

After a 7-10 day starvation period, the tortoise should be weighed.

weighed and then housed.

- The tortoise should be placed in a cardboard box lined with straw, with multiple air holes, which should be put inside a second cardboard box lined with straw and positioned in a dry, draught-free position.

  The reason for this is that it provides greater protection against frost damage, and, if a tortoise becomes too cold, it will dig downwards. The two boxes, therefore, help to contain the tortoise in a straw-insulated environment.

- The habitat should be placed in a cool room or building such as a garage which has a constant temperature. The environmental temperature should be kept between 4-10°C (39.2-50°F) for the whole of the hibernation period. Any lower than 4°C (39.2°F) and frost damage with

blindness and nervous system damage can occur; much higher than 10°C (50°F) and the tortoise will recover from hibernation.

SAFETY CHECKS

During the hibernation period, the tortoise should be checked once or twice weekly to see if there has been any movement, or recovery from hibernation. Once a month, reweigh the tortoise, as any loss of weight over a month greater than one per cent of body weight should be viewed as being abnormal and the tortoise should be recovered from hibernation. All of these procedures should be performed at 4-10°C (39.2-50°F).

Indoor hibernation tends to last from the end of October through until February. In general, once daytime temperatures regularly start getting above 10°C (50°F)

The hibernating tortoise should be placed in a box within a bigger box, for maximum protection against the frost.

the tortoise will revive, and it is important that the owner quickly detects the increased breathing movements and small muscular twitches which signify this.

OUTDOOR CARE

Outdoor hibernation does occur in certain temperate climates without problems. For example, seasoned tortoises in the south of England, which have plenty of cover in which to bury themselves from the frosts, will last for 5-6 months from October to April.

However, in general, this is not recommended in the colder northerly climes, particularly for the more sensitive Marginated and Tunisian/Middle Eastern Spur-Thighed subspecies.

POST-HIBERNATION

Once hibernation has been completed, or the tortoise has been aroused early due to a warm winter or medical intervention, he or she must be revived slowly but in a controlled manner. This means bringing the tortoise into a warmed environment and gradually increasing the environmental temperature over a 24-hour period from 10°C (50°F) up to the desired 20-26°C (68-78.8°F).

The tortoise's mouth, nose, eyes and vent should be cleaned in a shallow bath of lukewarm water. This helps it to open its eyes and often encourages it to eat, drink, defecate and urinate. The latter is important as it encourages the kidneys to excrete waste products which have built up over the winter.

The tortoise should be left in the bath for 30-45 minutes to allow it to warm up sufficiently and, hopefully, to drink in order to replenish its fluid balance.

Once active, the tortoise should be kept warm and offered plenty of foods with high water and energy content, such as steamed squashes, pumpkins, swedes, soaked alfalfa pellets, melons, apples, fresh figs etc.

This may require further retention in an indoor vivarium with supplementary lighting and heating, as the warmth and exposure to increasing periods of ultraviolet light act as appetite stimulants and tell the tortoise not to go back into hibernation.

It is vitally important that, once out of hibernation, the tortoise is not allowed to go back again that season. It will not have the energy reserves to do so and the risks of it dying in the process are high.

BEHAVIOUR

Beautiful and important creatures though tortoises are, they are not exactly nature's mental giants! Their brains are extremely small, and most of their lifestyle is a set response to a series of outside stimuli.

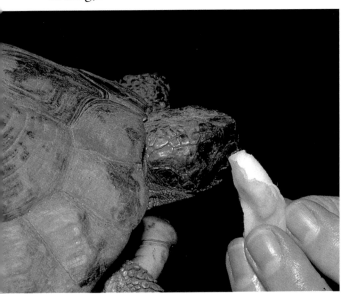

Clean the eyes, nose and mouth as the tortoise comes out of hibernation.

The adult tortoise will become active once its body has reached the optimum temperature.

ADULTS

A common daily routine is for the tortoise to emerge from the overnight resting place, and to bask in a prominent position in order to raise internal body temperature.

Once warmed sufficiently, the tortoise will then move off in search of food. Only when it is at the correct Preferred Body Temperature (PBT) will proper digestion and metabolism occur.

As the daytime temperature rises above the tortoise's ideal temperature range (known as the Preferred Optimum Temperature Zone (POTZ)), it will move into shade under vegetation or rocks, or dig a burrow. Once the heat of the day passes, the tortoise will often emerge to bask in the evening sun before retiring to a safe overnight shelter, secure from predators.

JUVENILES

Young tortoises differ from adults in that they are often in small groups or herds and stand a higher risk of predation. Their behaviour mirrors this, as they will tend to spend more of their time hiding, and so are commonly found burrowing.

You should provide a floor covering into which they can burrow, such as hay or straw, shredded newspaper or alfalfa pellets.

A juvenile tortoise is likely to spend more time in hiding.

In addition, many young tortoises in their first 3-4 years will dig burrows for themselves even during the middle of the summer and stay there for some weeks. This appears to be normal behaviour for many Mediterranean species, as they seem to be well fed, and resurface with no ill effects.

Note that no adult tortoises should do this during the summer; evidence of this behaviour suggests ill health.

PROBLEMS

Among the less aesthetically desirable behavioural traits of tortoises, especially the juvenile ones, is their predilection for consuming the faeces of other tortoises and indeed other species altogether.

This is thought to be a way of colonising their digestive system with the necessary bacteria and single-celled organisms on which tortoises rely for the digestion of the high-fibre foods they eat. It also means, however, that parasite problems such as worms can rapidly spread through a tortoise collection, and hence annual de-worming of pet tortoises is to be recommended.

ACCIDENTS

Tortoises are accident-prone. They are, as previously mentioned, not blessed with intelligence, and tend to try and walk through obstacles and danger rather than go around it. Many tortoises in captivity will drown in garden ponds, for example, and many others are injured in accidents with lawnmowers and strimmers every year. You must, therefore, think for the tortoise, and provide as danger-free an environment as possible.

6 *Nutrition*

All tortoises are herbivores. This may seem an obvious statement, but it is extremely important. The varieties of vegetables and fruits consumed by tortoises differ from species to species, but no tortoise consumes meat, even as a small fraction of their diet, on a regular basis in the wild. Some tortoises have been seen to consume carrion in the wild, but this is not normal behaviour.

NO MEAT

Some pet tortoises in the past were fed tinned dog or cat food as part of their staple diet. They would rapidly consume it and seemed to grow faster. The problem is that the side-effects of such a diet are life-threatening but, as with many diet-related problems, they take time to develop.

• Tinned foods are calorie-rich. The wild foods of many tortoises

In the past, tortoises were often fed tinned dog or cat food, but, in fact, the side effects of this type of diet are life-threatening.

involve grasses or fruits, both of which are not exactly full of calories! Their metabolism has adapted to this situation over millions of years, and so tortoises are meant to grow relatively slowly. If the calories are increased dramatically, then growth occurs too quickly. This exceeds the ability of the tortoise to calcify properly their rapidly growing shell and limbs, which may become extremely soft and flexible.

- If tinned foods which contain calcium are presented, the shell and limbs become misshapen and uneven.
- The excess fats presented in these foods lead to a rapid build-up of fat in the tortoise's body, which eventually leads to liver failure and the death of the tortoise.
- Tinned and fresh meat diets are extremely high sources of protein. The waste products of protein digestion are handled by the liver, which, in reptiles, produces the compound uric acid which is then excreted by the kidneys.

    Excess uric acid levels occur on these diets, which then form crystals in the bloodstream and the tortoise's internal organs.

This condition is known as visceral gout.

MASTICATION

Tortoises have no teeth. They eat by shearing off segments of their food with their hard, sharp beak, which is formed by a horny sheath to the jaw line. This is kept worn down by the consumption of fibrous foods, and abrasive contact with the rocky ground of their natural habitat.

In captivity, the feeding of too much soft food, especially off soft surfaces such as newspaper or straw, can lead to overgrowth of the beak. This then needs trimming back, otherwise the tortoises will very soon not be able to eat.

To prevent this from happening, it is important to feed some tough fibrous food types. It may also be useful to place some large smooth stones under the food when it is offered, as the tortoise will then scrape at these while trying to grab the food, so wearing down the beak.

DIGESTION

Once the food has entered the tortoise's mouth it is not chewed but simply swallowed in a gulping motion. All of the digestion and breakdown of the food occurs initially in the stomach and then in the intestines where fermentation and absorption occur.

WATER

Water is essential for life. It is claimed that tortoises do not need to drink, as they should obtain all of their water needs from their diet of leafy greens and fruit. This is partly true. In the wild, they feed off live fresh fruit and vegetable material.

However, in captivity, particularly in indoor vivaria, the food offered has already been cropped. This means that, as soon as it is placed into a heated tank, it starts to lose water and dehydrates. The tortoise, therefore, is imperceptibly, but chronically, denied water. Ultimately, kidney damage and gout is the result.

Fresh water *must* be provided on a daily basis. In particular, a tortoise will drink immediately after recovery from hibernation, and also during the fortnight before hibernation when it is not eating.

The water should be placed in heavy bowls which are difficult to tip over, and should be deep enough to submerge the tortoise's nose and mouth (generally 1-2 inches, 2-5 cms). As I have said before, tortoises do not have a hard palate so, to obtain the necessary suction for drinking, the nose as well as the mouth must be submerged. Fluid losses in reptiles average 10-25 millilitres per kilogram of body weight per day.

SUITABLE PLANTS

The Mediterranean, Indian and African species consume a mainly green, plant-based diet with occasional fruits and flowers.

Access to fresh drinking water is essential.

Much of the herbage and plant material found in their native environments is of a fibrous nature. Grasses, in particular, form a substantial part of the diet of the Leopard and African Spurred Tortoises, and their absence may cause digestive upsets.

In the Mediterranean species, the habitats are often in a loamy, high-calcium soil type, and this is reflected in the high calcium content of the plant material consumed. It therefore makes good sense to try and mimic this in captivity.

The South American tortoises may be fed much the same sort of fare, with the emphasis more on fruit and grasses, although they can be taught to consume any of the food types described here. Many of the more exotic species will also consume the more succulent cacti, such as prickly pears, or true succulents such as ice-plants.

- **Greens:** Kale, cabbage, cauliflower, spinach, watercress, fresh herbs such as flat-leaved parsley, basil, oregano, coriander, dandelion leaves, chicory, bok-choy, collard greens, swiss chard, clover (red for preference), garden weeds such as chickweed, charlock, plantains, vetches etc., small volumes of Romaine-type lettuce.

Kale is readily available and is generally eaten with relish.

- **Carbohydrate vegetables** (good for pre-hibernation/post-hibernation periods): Steamed squashes, pumpkin, carrot, sweet potatoes, parsnips, beetroot.
- **Fruits:** Apples, pears, strawberries, figs (fresh), melon, apricots, nectarines, peaches, plums, blackberries, papaya, mango, paw-paw, tomatoes, mandarin oranges.
- **Flowers:** Nasturtiums, roses, dandelions, courgette flowers.
- **Pulses:** Sprouted pulses such as mung beans are good.
- **Grasses and hay:** These are advocated for the African Spurred, the Leopard and the Horsfield's Tortoises. These three species in particular inhabit dry grasslands with a rocky terrain, and so seem to have a high requirement for the fibre these grasses produce.

It is important not to cut fresh grass and offer this, as it may rapidly ferment inside the tortoise and produce colic. Instead, allow them to graze on a lawned area, or provide them with the dried grass/hay products available commercially.

VARIETY
Variety is the spice of life as the saying goes, and the same should be applied to the feeding of tortoises. This avoids the problems of over-dependence on one food type which inevitably leads to an unbalanced diet.

This is particularly so with certain plant types, including the brassica family, such as Brussels sprouts, cabbage, kale and cauliflower. These contain 'goitregens' which bind up the iodine present in the diet, preventing the tortoise from obtaining it. The disease goitre then develops, which is manifested by a slow metabolism and fluid retention throughout the body, as well as increased susceptibility to infection.

Other plants which can be a problem are spinach, the tops of root crops such as beetroot and turnips, and the leaves of rhubarb. These all contain compounds known as oxalates which bind up the calcium in the diet and prevent the tortoise from obtaining it, leading to metabolic bone disease.

CAUTION
Excessive amounts of salad vegetables such as lettuce, cucumber and celery should not be fed to young tortoises, as these vegetables are mainly water with

little nutritional content and no calcium content for bone and shell growth. Other foods to avoid include bananas and kiwi fruits which are very sugary and can cause colic. Also avoid feeding avocados, as these are very high in fats which can cause liver damage in tortoises.

TORTOISE PELLETS

Several commercial pellet foods for tortoises are now available. These vary in their nutritional content and apparent palatability, but they do provide an easily stored homogenous food source. Their downfall is that they are still not well taken by tortoises and that little research has been done

Pellet food should be regarded as an additional source of food. It should always be well soaked before it is fed to a tortoise.

to assess their efficacy over several decades, which is how long some nutritional problems take to develop.

In general, it is recommended that pellets do not form the majority of the diet fed, but rather an additional food source. They should be fed well soaked in boiled, then cooled, water, as otherwise they swell inside the tortoise, causing gut blockages.

DIETARY PROBLEMS

CALCIUM AND VITAMIN D3

Probably the commonest problem for tortoises is a diet deficient in calcium, with or without a deficiency in vitamin D3.

Calcium is necessary for healthy bone growth, which includes the shell. It is also involved in a number of other essential processes in the body, such as blood clotting, the contraction of muscles etc.

For correct bone development to occur, calcium needs the vitamin D3, which helps by encouraging calcium absorption from the gut, and reabsorption from the urine passing through the kidneys, as well as regulating calcium deposition in the bones.

As previously mentioned, the

Mediterranean species in particular come from a calcium-rich geographic location, and so many of the plants they consume contain high levels of calcium.

This is combined with long exposure to unfiltered natural sunlight. It is the UVB rays in the sunlight that stimulate vitamin D3 production in the tortoise's skin. Hence, deficiencies in the wild are almost never seen.

In captivity, though, many tortoises are underexposed to sunlight due to the more northerly climes they are kept in, and lack of ultraviolet-providing light sources. Their diets may also be lacking in calcium, as in the all-salad-style cucumber, celery, iceberg lettuce diets.

For this reason, the provision of powdered calcium supplements is recommended, with or without vitamin D3 supplements.

The provision of a broad-spectrum light mimicking natural sunlight is also advised, which can provide the ultraviolet B rays needed for vitamin D3 synthesis, for those tortoises kept indoors.

These requirements are more especially needed for young, growing tortoises up to the age of ten years or so, particularly in the first 3-4 years of life.

VITAMIN A

Deficiency of this vitamin, or its vegetable precursors known as carotenes, causes a variety of problems. The most noticeable is the swelling of the region around the eyes, due to thickening and reduction in function of the tear glands.

There may also be a reduction in the production of saliva when feeding, with thickening of the lining of the mouth, and mouth infections becoming more common. A diet rich in a variety of leafy green vegetables with added roots such as carrot will prevent this from occurring.

A PROPER MENU

- Three-quarters of the diet to be composed of vegetable matter of a leafy nature such as dandelions, kale, watercress, flat-leaved parsley, chicory, bok-choy, peas, beans, hay/dried grass, fresh grass (not cut), grated carrot, grated pumpkin, sweet peppers etc.
- One-eighth of the diet to be composed of fruits such as apples, pears, melon, papaya, passion fruit, strawberries, plums etc.
- One-eighth of the diet to be composed of flowers such as

Hand-feeding will help to make your tortoise become more tame.

dandelions, nasturtiums, roses, and sprouted seeds such as mung beans, lentils etc.

• For more tropical species such as the Red- and Yellow-Footed Tortoises, the amount of fruit and flowers may be doubled.

• It is recommended that calcium supplementation be given by providing calcium lactate or gluconate on a daily basis, with a calcium/vitamin D3 supplement added once or twice weekly, depending on whether the tortoise is a juvenile (higher requirement) or an adult (lower requirement).

POISONOUS PLANTS

Allowing tortoises to wander freely in a well-populated garden may sound appealing, but you could be exposing them to potentially poisonous plants.

This is a very complex subject. For example, do you know that daffodils can be harmful? Find out more about this subject from your garden centre and from books detailing the various properties of shrubs, flowers and herbs and their effect on animals.

The most surprising plants can be toxic, so do your homework – and beware!

7 *Breeding Tortoises*

Pick a healthy, adult pair of tortoises of different sexes. This may sound like an obvious point, but the number of same-sex 'infertile pairs' of tortoises presented to reptile vets is still significant!

Most species do not become sexually mature until they are over seven years of age, so how old is your tortoise? Determining the age of tortoises is extremely difficult in captivity due to the possibility of erratic growth patterns affecting shell shape and overall size.

The proposed breeding pair need to be in good bodily condition. If they are too over- or underweight then the female will not produce eggs at all, or in the case of being overweight, may have difficulties passing the eggs.

Pick two tortoises of the same subspecies. Different species will not mate, but different subspecies within the species still can mate successfully, although reproductive success is often reduced. If different subspecies within the same species are to be bred, it is important not to use a male from a larger subspecies with a female from a smaller one. This will lead to larger eggs than normal for that female, and the risk of egg-binding.

PREPARATION

One of the most important points to consider is whether the species hibernates. If it does, then the pair must have had a normal hibernation during the previous winter for there to be a good chance of a successful mating.

This is because exposure to the normal annual rhythms of activity and hibernation appear to have a controlling effect on important glands within the tortoise body, such as the thyroid and the

A breeding pair of Elongated Tortoises. The tortoises should be kept separate until it is time to mate.

pituitary, and these, in turn, have a function in turning on the reproductive cycle, and stimulating the desire to mate.

It is advisable to keep the two sexes apart from each other during the rest of the year and then introduce them at mating time. This helps avoid over-familiarity, which in many species leads to a lack of interest between the two sexes. Some males, however, will pester the females out of season which can lead to stress – another reason for separating the sexes for the rest of the year.

TIMING

- Mediterranean species mate best immediately after coming out of hibernation, or in the early autumn after they have spent a long summer feeding.

- The Indian Starred Tortoise's mating season in its native habitat is at the start of the monsoon season, which approximates to late June through to September.

- The South American species (the Red-Legged, Yellow-Legged and Chaco Tortoises) seem to reproduce throughout the year, assuming they are kept under optimal conditions, although most often mating occurs during the winter months in their native habitat, and then laying of the eggs during the summer.

- The African Spurred and Leopard Tortoise species also seem to mate more frequently during the slightly cooler winter periods in their natural habitat. In captivity, assuming optimal conditions, they often breed all year round.

INTRODUCTIONS

Introduce the male of the species to the female's territory.

The pen should be heated to the correct temperature for that species. The lighting should also mimic the time of year in which the species breeds.

These two points may not need to be considered if the tortoises are kept outside, but poor northern summers are a big reason for low fertility/failure to mate, so some thought may need to be given to additional heat and light.

The female's pen should also have good laying facilities. These can vary from a mound of bark chippings to loose earth or sand. Whatever is provided needs to be kept slightly damp, and must allow the female tortoise the chance to dig a nest pit.

The Mediterranean African and Indian species all prefer a substrate which is drier and more earth-like.

The South American species seem to prefer damper conditions. The best chance of success is to provide peat or moss, and pile it deep enough so that the female tortoise can dig a suitable nest for the eggs.

COURTSHIP

This varies from species to species.

The Mediterranean species demonstrate similar activity. The males are aggressive during the breeding season and, if kept together, will frequently ram each other and bite each other's legs and head.

When placed with a female, the male will give chase, ramming her shell with his and attempting to bite her in order to make her stop. During this process the Hermann's male will bob his head up and down in front of the female after circling her a few times, as does the Horsfield's Tortoise.

The male Spur-Thighed Tortoise tends to perform more side-to-side head movements. If the female stops, then the male will attempt to mount her from behind, resting his front feet on her carapace, while curling his tail around hers to oppose their vents. The male phallus becomes engorged at this point and enters the female's cloaca through the vent and guides the sperm in.

During this process the male will often emit various noises. The Horsfield's Tortoise seems to make a high-pitched, squeaking noise; the Spur-Thighed Tortoise goes for deeper, grunting noises.

The African Spurred Tortoise can be aggressive with rival males.

The South American species perform slightly differently. The male Red-Legged Tortoise, for example, will stand side by side with the female, rather then head on, and perform the head-twitching movements. These movements involve a sideways movement of the head and then its return to the centre.

A receptive female will stand stock still, and the male will take this as a signal to continue. He will then circle the female and sniff at her tail base, and may make clucking noises similar to a domestic chicken.

If the female continues to remain motionless, the male will mount the female from behind in a similar manner to that of the Mediterranean species.

The Indian Starred Tortoise is much less aggressive. The male will approach the female from the front without any physical contact and, if she stops moving, he will circle her several times, sniffing her tail base. If she continues to respond, the male will mount the female from behind, and will give out low grunting noises during the mating process.

The Leopard Tortoise, and African Spurred Tortoises are more aggressive in their exploits. They exhibit fighting tussles between rival males, with shell ramming and attempting to turn over competitors.

The female is treated in a similar manner until she stops moving. Then, after some circling and scenting the air and the female's tail base, the male will attempt to mount her from behind. During the process of mating, the male will utter harsh cries.

FEMALE CARE

The female tortoise will start to form fertile eggs after a successful mating. These are then carried in her reproductive system for a variable period of time before being laid. The female may dig several nest sites before settling on the final spot.

The incubation of the eggs should be performed in a purpose-built incubator in northern climates. This involves carefully digging up the eggs laid by the female. A discussion on the types of incubator and techniques available are given below.

MEDITERRANEANS

The Mediterranean species may carry these eggs from anywhere from 4 weeks to 3-4 years! This is because some females are mated in the autumn, when they are due to go into hibernation. The eggs may therefore be carried right through to the next year. Others may not find the correct nest sites, and so will not lay the eggs because of this.

In addition, the female can store the sperm from a successful mating, eventually allowing fertilisation to occur many months, or years, after exposure to the male, a factor which makes identification of the father sometimes rather difficult!

Once laid, the eggs will hatch, for most Mediterranean species, in 8-12 weeks depending on the temperature at which they are incubated.

SOUTH AMERICANS

The South American species may also carry the eggs inside the female reproductive tract for a period of weeks, or for as long as the more normal few months.

- The eggs of the Red-Legged and Yellow-Legged tortoises are more normally laid in July to September in the wild, and

SPECIES	AVERAGE CLUTCH SIZE	AVERAGE INCUBATION TIME
Spur-Thighed Tortoise	2-8	78-84 days at 29-30°C (83-85°F)
Hermann's Tortoise	6-10	62-66 days at 27-30°C (80-85°F)
Marginated Tortoise	12-16	59-73 days at 29-30°C (83-85°F)
Horsfield's Tortoise	4-6	75-82 days at 27-31°C (80-86°F)

Table of clutch sizes and average egg hatching times for Mediterranean species

mating has frequently occurred the previous winter.

The female then often lays the eggs in deep moist leaf-litter, an average of 5-13 eggs being laid in a clutch. Hatching times take between 106-184 days at a temperature of 30°C. The humidity needs to be kept much higher during the incubation process than with the other species, being typically between 75-85 per cent.

The Chaco Tortoise, which inhabits a drier climate than the Red/Yellow-Legged varieties, often lays eggs between November and February in the wild, laying an average of 1-4 eggs which may take up to a year to hatch at 27-30°C.

• The Indian Starred Tortoise will lay 1-6 eggs on average 60-90 days after mating in a 12-20 centimetre (5-7 inches) deep nest in lightly dampened sandy soil. These eggs will hatch in 90-120 days at a temperature of 29-31°C (83-86°F). The egg shells of the Indian Starred Tortoise are much harder and thinner than their Mediterranean counterparts, and careful handling is required to prevent breaking them when transferring them to the incubator.

• The Leopard Tortoise will carry the eggs for 3-4 months after mating, and then will lay an average clutch size of between 5-30 eggs, making it one of the

The Leopard Tortoise is one of the most prolific, laying between 5 and 30 eggs.

more prolific species. These then have a variable hatching time of between 120-540 days! The more common average, though, is between 120-210 days.

- The African Spurred Tortoise carries the eggs after mating for similar periods as the Leopard Tortoise, and then lays an average clutch of 17-33 eggs. These then hatch on average between 118-212 days at 28°C.

INCUBATION

In the colder, northerly climes of the northern states of the USA, the UK and northern Europe, the incubation of eggs in an outside environment is not possible, due to the high temperatures required. It is therefore necessary to dig up the eggs once they have been laid by the female and transfer them to a purpose-built incubator for hatching.

When the eggs are retrieved from the nest site, particular care should be taken to maintain the same position of the egg in the incubator. The eggs should not be turned or touched during the incubation process as this can cause significant foetal mortality.

THE INCUBATOR

Incubators may be purchased from many reptile outlets, or from commercial poultry suppliers as the poultry industry uses them for chicken/turkey rearing. Alternatively, it is perfectly possible to manufacture one at home.

SPECIES	AVERAGE CLUTCH SIZE	AVERAGE INCUBATION TIME
Chaco Tortoise	1-4	120-290 days at 27-30°C (80-85°F)
Red-Footed Tortoise	5-13	106-184 days at 30°C (85°F)
Yellow-Footed Tortoise	2-10	125-150 days at 27-28°C (80-82°F)
Indian Starred Tortoise	1-6	90-120 days at 29-31°C (83-86°F)
Leopard Tortoise	5-30	150-210 days at 28°C (82°F)
African Spurred Tortoise	17-33	118-212 days at 28°C (82°F)

Table comparing non-Mediterranean species' average clutch sizes and incubation times

*Many of the species listed above may achieve two clutches in the one season.

You need to start with a plastic, perspex, or toughened glass tank, with a plastic lid which contains aeration holes which can be covered to regulate humidity and temperature.

The next stage is to consider the substrate or nesting material in which to place the eggs. A useful medium is the loft-insulating material called vermiculite. Alternatives include damp sand, or sphagnum moss or even peat. This substrate is placed into small open containers within the tank, and the eggs are placed in slight depressions within the substrate.

The incubator needs to produce humidity and heat. There are two ways of doing this.

The small open containers containing the eggs and substrate may be placed on to a wire mesh which divides the tank into a top

The eggs will need to be transferred to an incubator for hatching.

and bottom compartment. The bottom compartment may then be three-quarters filled with filtered water, with a thermostatically controlled water heater placed in it. This technique will provide heat and moisture, and is good for species requiring higher moisture, such as the Red- and Yellow-Footed tortoises which need an average 80 per cent humidity.

An alternative set-up is to have a radiant heat mat attached to the outside of the tank, which is thermostatically controlled. The inside is then completely filled with the substrate, which is kept moist by regular misting with a plant sprayer, and by placing shallow containers of filtered and previously boiled water in among the eggs.

This provides a drier atmosphere, more suited for the African species, although care should be taken not to allow the humidity to drop below 50 per cent, as the tortoise eggs are porous, and excessively dry conditions will dehydrate the foetus inside and lead to high levels of mortality.

SEX-DETERMINATION

As with many reptiles, tortoise sex determination depends on the temperature at which the eggs were incubated. For example, the Spur-Thighed Tortoise will produce males if the eggs are kept at 29.5°C (84°F) and females if kept at 31.5°C (88°F).

It seems that this fact can be applied to a large number of other

A family of Leopard Tortoises: Sex-determination depends on the temperature at which the eggs are incubated.

tortoise species, with males being predominantly produced at the lower temperatures, and females at the higher ones. Therefore, it can be seen that if the temperature range is from 28-31°C (81-86°F), a mixture of sexes is likely to be achieved.

HATCHLINGS

The tortoise hatchling emerges from its shell by piercing the inside with its 'egg tooth', which is a sharp spur on its nose-tip.

Tortoise egg shells are generally more leathery than a chicken's and consequently softer. This has a downside in that they are more prone to dehydration/ overhydration during incubation,

but it makes them slightly easier to escape from at hatching time.

Some species immediately crawl away from the egg in search of food; others, such as the Red- and Yellow-Footed species, may remain within the opened shell for 2-3 days before emerging.

This is often necessary to allow the final absorption of the yolk sac which provides the nutrition for the tortoise inside the egg, and which may still be seen to protrude from the mid-portion of the hatchling's plastron.

It is important that the tortoise is protected within the remains of its shell if this yolk sac is still present after hatching. Rupture of the sac due to trauma can cause

Baby tortoises should be kept inside a heated vivarium to safeguard them from disease.

significant loss of nutrition, infection, and also the escape of yolk into the abdomen of the tortoise, inducing peritonitis.

As soon as the hatchlings are out of their shells and starting to move away, they should be transferred to a separate vivarium heated to their optimum temperature range, and immediately provided with fresh leafy greens.

YOUNGSTERS

Young tortoises should always be kept in a heated vivarium. It has been found that they are especially prone to diseases if they are not kept within their preferred optimum temperature zone.

Their care is otherwise similar to adults, except that calcium and vitamin D3 supplementation is particularly necessary for the rapid bone and shell growth which occurs.

This is best given as a daily calcium powder supplement, with a combined calcium/vitamin D3 supplement given twice weekly.

In addition, the presence of an artificial sunlight light source, providing ultraviolet light, should be available inside the tank.

This will allow the growing tortoises to manufacture their own source of vitamin D3.

Calcium and vitamin D3 deficiencies are the biggest causes of growth deformities in young

Young Marginated Tortoise: Calcium and vitamin supplementation is essential during rapid bone and shell growth.

tortoises, especially the larger and faster-growing breeds such as the Leopard and African Spurred Tortoises.

REPRODUCTIVE PROBLEMS
These can be many and varied. They include the following:
• Incompatible parents (wrong ages, wrong sex, wrong species).
• Malnourished parents which will lead to a failure to mate.
• Overweight parents which may lead to poor reproductive performance and a greater risk of the eggs becoming stuck inside the female.

Other problems include a failure to lay the eggs (egg-binding) because of a lack of a suitable nest site or nest material. This may also occur because of too cold an environmental temperature, or a poor diet, such as the lack of calcium-rich foods.

The production of egg shells withdraws large amounts of calcium from the tortoise's bloodstream and skeletal tissues, and is usually replaced by calcium from the diet.

If this is not provided, then the supply of calcium from the bones often cannot keep pace with the demand from the egg production, and blood calcium levels fall.

The final outcome is an extremely sick tortoise, unable to lay her eggs (which in themselves are occupying a restricted space, so reducing the room for the digestive contents and hence appetite) and rapidly deteriorating into a state of shock and death.

Other difficulties include the formation of deformed eggs which can become too large to be passed through the narrow vent bounded by the carapace and plastron.

Large eggs may result from the mating of a larger subspecies such as the Iranian (*Testudo graeca zarudnyi*) or Asia Minor (*Testudo graeca iberis*) Spur-Thighed Tortoise with the smaller subspecies Middle Eastern (*Testudo graeca terrestris*) Spur-Thighed Tortoise.

Eggs may also take a different route out of the reproductive system. Because the reproductive system and urinary systems both empty into the same part of the cloaca (the common exit of the digestive, reproductive, and urinary systems) before exiting the body through the vent, an egg may actually reverse itself and enter the tortoise's bladder, where it may become infected and cause disease.

The female tortoise may also push out part of her reproductive system (known as a prolapse) by

Breeding tortoises can be rewarding, but it demands considerable expertise.

straining too hard when laying. This requires veterinary attention, as do most reproductive difficulties. Surgery may be necessary to replace the prolapse, and is frequently needed to remove eggs in cases of egg-binding, or with oversized or deformed eggs.

8

Health Care

A sick tortoise will show one or more symptoms. These can be varied, but several common factors should alert the conscientious tortoise owner to seek veterinary attention.

WARNING SIGNS

- Unexplained weight loss: for example, the tortoise which is steadily losing weight during the summer months.
- Loss of appetite (other than that associated with the pre-hibernation fasting of Mediterranean species).
- Perpetually hiding in the corners of the garden or the vivarium during the middle of the summer.
- Evidence of upper airway disease such as a runny nose, foamy saliva-like material in the mouth, or obvious mouth-breathing (tortoises should breathe through their noses).

- Evidence of diarrhoea. Tortoise faeces should be pellet-shaped and relatively firm.
- Tortoises should never be sick; any vomiting is a severe sign and veterinary advice should be immediately sought.

If you keep a close check on your tortoise you will spot any signs of trouble at an early stage.

- Any damage to the shell is important as this is living tissue. Trauma to it allows infectious organisms access to the tortoise's body. Open wounds can become rapidly infected by environmental bacteria and develop abscesses.
- Head tilts, walking in perpetual small circles or obvious lack of use of one or more legs should be investigated. A lack of response to your touch is another obvious indication of a seriously unwell tortoise.
- Continual straining to pass something through the vent, but with no evidence of any egg or faeces, should alert you to the possibility of retained eggs in a female tortoise. Males may prolapse their penis due to chronic wasting diseases or straining due to gut parasites. This large, fleshy organ can become quickly and seriously damaged if not put back in its proper place.

COMMON DISEASES

For all of the following conditions it is important that you seek qualified veterinary advice. Make sure you find a veterinary surgeon who is used to dealing with reptiles on a regular basis.

SHELL PROBLEMS

Ulceration and infection of the shell is not uncommon, particularly when tortoises are kept in wetter conditions than they are biologically adapted to.

In terrestrial tortoises, the shell is frequently affected by bacterial disease in wet conditions, a condition known as 'shell rot'. Individual scales may lift off the carapace or plastron and expose weeping reddened areas underneath. In severe cases, the bone of the shell may be exposed and infected, which can lead to septicaemia, allowing the infection to reach internal organs and cause serious life-threatening conditions.

These shell infections are more common in the dry-loving Mediterranean species, particularly the Horsfield's Tortoises, and the African and Indian species. The South American species cope better with damp environmental conditions.

Cracked shells may occur due to trauma, such as lawnmower injuries, or because of being dropped. Or they may be due to infection of the shell.

SKIN AILMENTS

Skin swellings may arise anywhere on the body or limbs of a tortoise.

Some can be due to infestations of maggots from blow-flies. These can be a serious problem in outdoor tortoises in mid-summer, particularly those suffering from weeping skin wounds, or diarrhoea.

The flies are attracted to the odour of these conditions and lay their eggs on the skin surface of the tortoise. Within hours, the eggs hatch into maggots which start to eat their way into the tortoise; it is a horrible condition.

Other swellings may be due to infections from wounds, or thorn penetrations, which cause an abscess to form. In mammals, an abscess is filled with a liquid material (pus); reptiles produce a solid form of this. An example of this is the ear abscess seen in some tortoises, whereby infection occurs in the middle ear. Tortoises have no outer ear, only the eardrum

flush with the skin of the head, and the infected middle ear lies behind this. The abscess therefore causes protrusion of the eardrum, appearing as a swelling on the side of the tortoise's head.

BEAKS

Overgrown beaks can be another common problem, often arising in tortoises being fed softer foods, or eating off smooth surfaces. In the wild, the constant biting on dry and brittle vegetation, or the scraping of the beak on hard ground to pick up food, promotes proper wearing of the beak. If the beak is not worn down quickly enough, it overgrows and so needs to be trimmed manually. Some overgrown beaks are also associated with diets poor in calcium/vitamin D3, and are actually another manifestation of metabolic bone disease.

In the wild, the beak wears down naturally.

If the environment is below the optimum temperature, health problems will result.

DEFORMITIES

Soft or deformed shells are another common presentation in young growing tortoises on calcium- and vitamin D3-deficient diets. As already mentioned, rapidly growing animals need plenty of these two nutrients to keep their shells and bones hard and calcified as they grow. If there is too little, then the shell does not mineralise and so becomes softened. This can lead to deformities, as the muscles attaching to the underside of the shell can bend the shell, making it lumpy. In some tortoises, a series of pyramids may be produced across the carapace, which is thought to be due to a combination of an excess of dietary protein, with a relative lack of calcium. It may be seen in tortoises fed on animal proteins such as chicken.

BREATHING PROBLEMS

Runny noses may be seen in many tortoises, especially the Mediterranean species, being particularly severe in Marginated Tortoises. The condition is caused by a number of bacteria and may be exacerbated by a herpes virus associated with ulcerative stomatitis (see below).

Its real significance is that, as tortoises breathe through their noses, a lot of the bacteria are then sucked down into the tortoise's lungs and can start pneumonia. In addition, tortoises rely on their sense of smell to encourage their appetite, so those affected are frequently anorexic.

Runny nose syndrome is often associated with sub-optimal environmental conditions, such as a bout of cold weather, a failure in tank heating etc. It may also be connected with a lack of vitamin A in the tortoise's diet, as this vitamin is important for the functioning of the local immune system of the airways and gut, as well as for the normal functioning of saliva and tear glands.

Mouth-breathing and gasping for air can indicate a serious lung and lower airway problem. This may well be a sequel to the runny nose syndrome, but can also occur due to parasites, such as some intestinal worms which will migrate through the tortoise's liver and lungs as they mature before finally ending up in the gut. In any case, the tortoise will not eat and has its head outstretched, with its mouth open and gasping for air. Often there is an excess of frothy fluid in the mouth or from the nostrils. Again, poor husbandry and/or environmental conditions can exacerbate or bring on this condition.

DIGESTIVE PROBLEMS

Oral ulceration, also known as infectious stomatitis, is a condition blamed on a herpes virus seen commonly in Mediterranean species, often after recovery from hibernation. It may also be caused by bacterial infections and frequently stops the tortoise from eating. This can lead to further debilitation and other conditions such as septicaemia may develop.

DIARRHOEA

Diarrhoea is a not-uncommon problem in tortoises. It can be associated with heavy parasitism due to single-celled organisms known collectively as 'flagellates'. This condition is highly infectious and can sweep through a herd of tortoises very quickly. It causes anorexia, often diarrhoea or the passing of undigested food, and severe intestinal damage which can be irreversible. Other causes include a family of single-celled parasites known as 'ciliates' which can cause severe large intestine damage. They are particularly dangerous to hatchling tortoises and cause severe diarrhoea and dehydration.

Diarrhoea is highly infectious, so tortoises living together will be at risk.

CONSTIPATION

Constipation may occur due to the consumption of 'foreign bodies' such as stones, sand, soil etc. This is a common problem in tortoises on a calcium-poor diet, as they strive to obtain more minerals from their environment. It is also associated with intestinal parasitism, in an apparent attempt to assuage the discomfort caused.

Constipation may also be a sequel to dehydration from other factors, or from the less common possibility of cancer. Some of the gut parasites, such as the tortoise roundworm *Angusticaecum* spp. can cause a blockage of the gut if present in large enough numbers. This is one of the reasons for advising tortoise owners to get their tortoises de-wormed on an annual basis after checking the faeces for signs of the microscopic worm eggs. Intestinal worms can also cause weight loss and anaemia, which may result in the tortoise appearing dull and lethargic.

ANOREXIA

Anorexia is not so much a disease as the result of a disease. It therefore has many possible causes. One specific condition observed in Mediterranean species is the disease known as Post Hibernational Anorexia (PHA). This syndrome is seen, as its name suggests, immediately after recovery from hibernation.

The tortoise affected also frequently has a low weight to length ratio (Jackson's Ratio) and also may be suffering from infectious stomatitis or runny nose syndrome.

Normally on awakening from hibernation, the tortoise's blood sugar levels rise dramatically, which triggers its appetite. In sick, diseased or underweight tortoises this does not happen, and so the tortoise will not eat. This leads to progressive dehydration and the tortoise starts to lose weight dramatically as it burns up body tissues for energy.

It is essential that veterinary attention is sought if the following home therapies are not working.
• Warm the tortoise to the correct temperature.
• Bathe it regularly to clean its eyes and nose, and to encourage drinking, defecating and urinating.
• Assist feeding by placing food in the tortoise's mouth.

COLIC

Colic can be caused by parasitic

Observe your tortoise closely when it comes out of hibernation to ensure it is eating properly.

conditions. The tortoise is uncomfortable and may kick at the sides of its shell, or be anorexic and bloated in appearance. Colic can also be caused by the feeding of inappropriate food substances such as sugary fruits like bananas, or the feeding of dairy products, where the milk sugar lactose causes excess gas production.

VOMITING

This is very serious. It may be associated with gut blockages or septicaemia.

LIVER PROBLEMS

Fatty liver disease can occur due to feeding the tortoise cat and dog foods, leading to excess fat deposits which affect the liver function, causing liver failure. This may present as a number of conditions, varying from neurological signs through to anorexia and weight loss.

NEUROLOGICAL INDICATIONS

Head tilts and circling when walking can be due to frost damage to the brain. This injures the balance centres and so causes 'vestibular disease' whereby the tortoise is unable to orientate itself. The same problems may be associated with poisoning, septicaemia or liver damage.

Leg paralysis may occur for a number of reasons. It may affect a single limb, in which case infections and fractures are more common causes, or it may involve multiple limbs. The latter may be due to spinal cord damage due to trauma or infection if the hind limbs are affected. It may equally be due to a bladder stone, or retained eggs putting pressure on the nerves supplying the hind limbs. Other causes include egg-binding where low blood calcium results in muscular paralysis, or poisoning.

LAMENESS

Lameness may also be due to metabolic bone disease, causing weak and easily fractured bones. It may also be due to swollen joints, such as those caused by infections, or by a condition known as articular gout. This is where uric acid crystals, which are the waste product of protein metabolism, are produced in excess due to a high-protein diet, or are not excreted from the body due to kidney/circulation failure, and so they will precipitate out into the body. This can occur around the internal organs such as the heart, liver and kidneys causing damage to their function, or, alternatively, the crystals may form in the joints causing pain and inflammation.

EYES

Swollen eyes can be due to infections of the eye, often secondary to infections of the nose and sinuses of the head. The problem may also be due to a lack of vitamin A in the diet. This condition causes a thickening of the glands responsible for producing tears. Consequently no tears are produced and the eye becomes inflamed and prone to infection.

A white opacity can appear in the outer layer of the eye (the cornea) in tortoises as they age. It is a deposition of cholesterol and is known as 'arcus lipoides corneae'.

Blindness may occur as a sequel to frost damage during hibernation. It can also occur after infections due to vitamin A deficiencies and upper airway disease, as well as straightforward severe conjunctivitis.

ZOONOTIC DISEASES

The definition of a zoonotic disease is one which can be passed from animals to man. Tortoises can pass on diseases to humans.

The important zoonotic disease

With good care and management, your tortoise should live a long life, and suffer few health problems.

is Salmonellosis. This is the series of bacterial gut, or indeed skin infections, associated with the bacteria *Salmonella spp.* There are many bacteria within this family, some being more serious than others.

It is known that the majority of tortoises carry some form of *Salmonella spp.* bacteria within their digestive system, even though the individual tortoise may show no evidence of disease at all. It is important to appreciate that you cannot eradicate *Salmonella spp.* totally from a tortoise so affected, and indeed it may not be desirable to do so as this increases the risks of it developing antibiotic resistance.

Every tortoise should be viewed as a potential carrier of Salmonellosis, and so maximum hygiene precautions should be employed when handling them. This includes ensuring that hands are thoroughly washed after handling a tortoise, and that tortoises should not be allowed to wander freely over floors which young children will then crawl across. Young children should be discouraged from playing with tortoises, and on no account should tortoises be allowed into a food preparation area.

Finally, all human beings who are immunosuppressed due to diseases such as diabetes mellitus, AIDS, leukaemia, those on immunosuppressive medication such as corticosteroids or chemotherapy, the very young and the elderly, should be particularly aware of the risks of contracting Salmonellosis from tortoises.